WN 12\15

WITHDRAWN
FOR BOOKSALE

8/12 NSPL

Please return/renew this item by the last date shown.

To renew this item, call **0845 0020777** (automated)
or visit **www.librarieswest.org.uk**

Borrower number and PIN required.

Libraries**West**

The Women's Institute

the**WI**
INSPIRING WOMEN

traditional
favourites

SIMON &
SCHUSTER
ILLUSTRATED

London · New York · Sydney · Toronto · New Delhi

A CBS COMPANY

First published in Great Britain by
Simon & Schuster UK Ltd, 2012
A CBS Company

Simon & Schuster Illustrated Books,
Simon & Schuster UK Ltd,
222 Gray's Inn Road, London WC1X 8HB

www.simonandschuster.co.uk

Simon & Schuster Australia, Sydney
Simon & Schuster India, New Delhi

Editorial Director: **Francine Lawrence**
Senior Commissioning Editor: **Nicky Hill**
Project Editor: **Nicki Lampon**
Designer: **Richard Proctor**
Photographer: **William Shaw**
Stylist and Art Direction: **Tony Hutchinson**
Home Economist: **Sara Lewis**
Commercial Director: **Ami Richards**
Production Manager: **Katherine Thornton**

Colour reproduction by Dot Gradations Ltd, UK
Printed and bound in China

A CIP catalogue record for this book is available
from the British Library.

ISBN 978-1-47110-178-6

Notes on the recipes

Both metric and imperial measurements have
been given in all recipes. Use one set of
measurements only and not a mixture of both.
Spoon measures are level and 1 tablespoon =
15 ml, 1 teaspoon = 5 ml.

Preheat ovens before use and cook on the centre
shelf unless cooking more than one item. If using
a fan oven, reduce the heat by 10–20°C, but
check with your handbook.

Medium eggs have been used unless otherwise
stated.

This book contains recipes made with nuts. Those
with known allergic reactions to nuts and nut
derivatives, pregnant and breast-feeding women
and very young children should avoid these
dishes.

Recipes in this book were first published in 2002
under the titles *Best-kept Secrets of the Women's
Institute: Low Calorie Home Cooking, Best-kept
Secrets of the Women's Institute: Healthy Heart,
Best-kept Secrets of the Women's Institute:
Healthy Fast Food, Best-kept Secrets of the
Women's Institute: Home Cooking, Best-kept
Secrets of the Women's Institute: Puddings &
Desserts* and *Best-kept Secrets of the Women's
Institute: Breads & Bakes.*

Contents

Introduction

Most of us love a homemade pie – crumbly pastry covering a delicious savoury or sweet filling – or a traditional crumble with soft fruit and a crunchy topping, or even a simple salad with classic, fresh ingredients. Traditional favourites.

Traditional food doesn't have to mean boring food. Too often we think of classics as old-fashioned and dull, but with a great recipe these dishes can be just as wonderful and tasty as any fancy modern recipe. Classic dishes have become classics just because so many people have enjoyed them for so many years. Add a little modern twist and even an everyday steak and kidney pie can become something extra special. Use good ingredients, such as lean cuts of meat and seasonal fruit and vegetables, and you are sure to produce a winner every time.

From classic salads to pasta dishes, delicious pies and scrumptious desserts, this book is packed full of favourite recipes from the Women's Institute. Renowned for their cooking expertise, there is no one better to produce a book of traditional favourites. With something here for a variety of occasions, many of these recipes are quick and easy to cook after a busy working day. Others are perfect for days when you have a little more time to let something slowly simmer on the hob or bake gently in the oven. Try them out on your family or dish them up when you are entertaining, there really is no reason not to enjoy traditional favourites every day of the week.

Nothing beats home cooking and every home cook needs a repertoire of traditional, fail-proof classics. This is it, so pick a favourite and get cooking.

Starters
& snacks

Niçoise salad

Make double the amount of French dressing. It will keep in the fridge in a screw top jar for at least 3 weeks.

Serves 4
Preparation and
cooking time:
40 minutes

100 g (3½ oz) **French beans**, trimmed and halved

2 **Little Gem lettuces** or
1 **Cos lettuce**, chopped

4 **tomatoes**, each cut into eight

½ small **red onion**, very finely sliced

175 g can **tuna in brine**, very well drained and flaked into large chunks

2 **hard boiled eggs**, quartered

8–10 **black** or **green olives**

chopped fresh **parsley**, to garnish

French dressing
4 tablespoons **olive oil**
1 tablespoon **cider vinegar**
or **tarragon vinegar**
a good pinch of **caster sugar**
1 **garlic clove**, crushed
1 teaspoon **French mustard**

Bring a small saucepan of water to the boil and add the beans. Bring back to the boil, cook for 1 minute, drain and immediately rinse the beans in cold water.

Arrange the lettuce on a large serving dish. Add the cooked beans, the tomatoes, onion and tuna.

Lay the eggs and olives on top. Then, with very clean hands, gently mix the salad together.

Put all the dressing ingredients into a screw top jar, screw on the lid and shake well.

When ready to serve, toss with the dressing and sprinkle with the parsley.

Asparagus quiche

Fresh asparagus and Gruyère cheese combine well to make a subtle filling for this delicious quiche.

Serves 4
Preparation time:
20 minutes +
30 minutes chilling
Cooking time:
50–55 minutes

Wholemeal pastry
115 g (4¼ oz) **wholemeal flour**
1 teaspoon **baking powder**
25 g (1 oz) **butter** or **block margarine**, cubed
25 g (1 oz) **white vegetable fat**, cubed

Filling
80 g (3 oz) **asparagus tips**
80 g (3 oz) **Gruyère cheese**, grated
2 large **eggs**, plus 1 **egg yolk**
250 ml (9 fl oz) **semi-skimmed milk**
½ teaspoon **Dijon mustard**
freshly ground **black pepper**

Mix the flour and baking powder together in a bowl and rub in the butter or margarine and vegetable fat until the mixture resembles fine breadcrumbs. Sprinkle over 2 tablespoons of cold water and bring it together to form a ball of dough.

Roll out the pastry thinly on a lightly floured surface, and use it to line a deep 20 cm (8 inch) flan tin. Prick the base with a fork and chill for at least 30 minutes. Preheat the oven to 200°C/400°F/Gas Mark 6 and place a baking tray on the middle shelf.

Line the pastry case with a sheet of foil, greaseproof paper or non-stick baking parchment and fill with baking beans. Bake blind for 15 minutes. Remove the lining and beans and return to the oven for a further 5 minutes, until lightly golden.

Meanwhile, bring a saucepan of water to the boil and blanch the asparagus tips for 2 minutes. Drain and plunge them into cold water to stop them from cooking.

Remove the pastry case from the oven and reduce the temperature to 190°C/375°F/Gas Mark 5.

Scatter the grated cheese over the base of the pastry case. Whisk together the eggs, egg yolk, milk and mustard and season with black pepper. Pour the mixture over the cheese. Drain the asparagus and arrange the tips on top.

Return the quiche to the oven and bake for 30–35 minutes, until puffy and golden. Serve warm or cold.

Smoked chicken Waldorf

This is a take on the classic Waldorf salad. Smoked chicken has a really good flavour, but you could substitute cold cooked chicken if preferred.

Serves 4
Preparation time:
  20 minutes

1 **head of celery**, cut into
  chunks
2 **red skinned apples**,
  quartered and cored
50 g (1¾ oz) **walnut pieces**
200 g (7 oz) **smoked chicken
  breast**, cut into bite-size
  pieces
3 tablespoons **French
  dressing** (see page 8)
2 tablespoons chopped
  fresh **parsley**, to garnish

Put the celery in a large bowl. Cut the apple quarters in half again, and cut each piece into four or five chunks. Add to the celery.

Add the walnuts, chicken and French dressing and stir to mix well. Pile on to pretty plates, sprinkle over the parsley and serve immediately.

Classic Caesar salad

No salt is needed here because the anchovy essence is salty. Croûtons will keep well in a tin, so cook more than you need and use to garnish soups.

Serves 4
Preparation time:
  15 minutes
Cooking time:
  20 minutes

2 thick slices **wholemeal**
  or **granary bread**, crusts
  removed and cut into
  small cubes
100 g (3½ oz) **crème fraîche**
1 **garlic clove**, crushed
a squeeze of **lemon juice**
1 dessertspoon **anchovy**
  essence
freshly ground **black pepper**
1 **Cos lettuce** or 2 **Little Gem**
  lettuces, roughly chopped
50 g (1¾ oz) **Parmesan**
  cheese, grated

Preheat the oven to 180°C/350°F/Gas Mark 4.

To make the croûtons, put the bread cubes on a baking tray and bake for about 20 minutes until completely dry and crispy.

Put the crème fraîche in a small bowl and mix in the garlic, lemon juice and anchovy essence. Season with black pepper.

Put the lettuce in a deep bowl. When you are ready to serve, pour over the crème fraîche dressing, mix well and sprinkle over the croûtons and grated Parmesan.

Sticky glazed drumsticks

A supremely simple but tasty way to liven up chicken drumsticks or thighs. Equally delicious served hot or cold.

Serves 4
Preparation time:
 15 minutes + 1 hour marinating
Cooking time:
 25–30 minutes

8 **chicken drumsticks** or **thighs**, or a mixture of each, skin removed

Marinade
grated zest and juice of an **orange**
2 tablespoons **clear honey**
2 tablespoons **olive oil**
½ teaspoon **ground ginger**
½ teaspoon **ground cumin**
1 tablespoon **orange marmalade**
freshly ground **black pepper**

Whisk together all the ingredients for the marinade, ensuring that the marmalade is well broken up.

Place the chicken pieces in a shallow dish. Pour the marinade over and turn them to coat well. Place in the fridge and leave for at least 1 hour to allow the flavours to develop.

Preheat the oven to 180ºC/350°F/Gas Mark 4. Remove the chicken pieces from the marinade and place in a shallow roasting tin. Drizzle over a little of the marinade and then discard the rest.

Roast the chicken pieces for 25–30 minutes until thoroughly cooked. When the chicken is pierced, any juices that run out should be completely clear and not tinged with pink. Serve hot or cold.

Lamb shish kebabs

A traditional Middle Eastern dish, 'shish' kebab is a popular takeaway of spit-roasted lamb, sliced and served in pitta bread.

Serves 4
Preparation time:
  20 minutes +
  overnight marinating
Cooking time:
  20 minutes

450 g (1 lb) **lamb neck** or
  shoulder fillet, trimmed
  of all visible fat
2 fresh **rosemary sprigs**,
  bruised
1 **garlic clove**, thinly sliced
1 tablespoon **olive oil**
1 tablespoon **lemon juice**
freshly ground **black pepper**

To serve
4 **plain** or **wholemeal pitta**
  breads
½ **Cos** or **Romaine lettuce**,
  shredded
2 ripe **tomatoes**, diced
1 small **red onion**, thinly
  sliced
houmous or **tzatziki**

Place the lamb fillets in a bowl with the rosemary and garlic. Pour over the oil and lemon juice. Season with pepper and stir thoroughly to coat the meat. Cover and leave to marinate overnight if possible. Stir a couple of times.

Preheat the oven to 240°C/475°F/Gas Mark 9. Place a roasting tin in the oven on the highest shelf.

Scrape the rosemary leaves and garlic off the lamb. Place the fillets in the preheated roasting tin, taking care as the meat may spit. Cook for 20 minutes. Remove from the oven and allow the lamb to rest for 10 minutes.

Lightly toast or warm the pitta breads. Split them horizontally and fill with the lettuce, tomatoes and onion. Thinly slice the lamb and divide it between the pockets. Add some houmous or tzatziki to each pocket and serve at once.

Artichoke & salami pizza

Serves 3
**Preparation and
   cooking time:
   1 hour**

225 g (8 oz) **strong white
   bread flour**
1 teaspoon **easy-blend dried
   yeast**
½ teaspoon **coarse sea salt**
1 tablespoon **olive oil**

Topping
2 teaspoons **extra virgin
   olive oil**
150 ml (5 fl oz) **passata**
1 **garlic clove**, chopped
   finely
15 g (½ oz) fresh **basil
   leaves**, a few reserved to
   garnish and the rest torn
½ × 390 g can **artichoke
   hearts**, drained and halved
115 g (4¼ oz) **button
   mushrooms**, sliced
25 g (1 oz) **Italian salami with
   peppercorns**, slices halved
125 g (4½ oz) **buffalo
   mozzarella**, sliced thinly
½ small **red onion**, sliced
   thinly
12 **black olives**
15 g (½ oz) **Parmesan cheese**
   shavings, to garnish

Combine the flour, yeast and salt in a bowl. Make a well in the centre and pour in the oil and 150 ml (5 fl oz) of warm water. Mix to combine and then tip out on to a work surface and knead for 10 minutes until the dough is smooth. Place in an oiled polythene bag, in a warm place, for about 15 minutes.

Preheat the oven to 220°C/425°F/Gas Mark 7. Grease a baking tray.

Either roll out the dough on a lightly floured work surface or shape with your hands into a 30 cm (12 inch) round. Place on the baking tray and brush lightly with 1 teaspoon of the oil.

Smooth the passata evenly over the surface and scatter with the garlic and basil. Top with the remaining ingredients.

Cover loosely with an oiled polythene bag and leave in a warm place for 15 minutes to enable the dough to puff up slightly.

Remove the bag and drizzle the remaining teaspoon of oil over the pizza. Bake in the centre of the oven for 15–20 minutes. Check after 15 minutes and dab off any liquid that has come out of the mushrooms with a little kitchen towel. Return to the oven for a further 5 minutes if you like a crisp pizza.

Serve garnished with the Parmesan shavings and reserved basil sprigs.

Cornish pasties

Pasties are a classic example of how just a few good-quality ingredients can achieve a delicious result. They are best eaten warm.

Makes 6
Preparation time:
25 minutes
Cooking time:
40 minutes

Pastry
80 g (3 oz) **butter** or
   block margarine, cubed
80 g (3 oz) **white vegetable**
   fat, cubed
350 g (12 oz) **plain flour**
1 **egg**, beaten, to glaze

Filling
350 g (12 oz) **steak mince**
175 g (6 oz) **potato**, peeled,
   very thinly sliced and
   roughly chopped
175 g (6 oz) **turnip**, peeled,
   very thinly sliced and
   roughly chopped
1 **onion**, finely chopped
¼ teaspoon **dried mixed**
   herbs
a good pinch of **cayenne**
   pepper
sea salt and freshly ground
   black pepper

Preheat the oven to 220°C/425°F/Gas Mark 7. Lightly grease a baking tray.

For the pastry, rub the butter or margarine and vegetable fat into the flour until the mixture resembles fine breadcrumbs. Sprinkle over 6 tablespoons of cold water and bring it all together to form a ball of dough. Wrap in cling film and chill in the fridge while you make the filling.

In a bowl, combine the mince, potato, turnip and onion. Add the herbs and cayenne pepper and season. Stir in 2 tablespoons of cold water to moisten.

Divide the pastry into six. On a lightly floured surface, roll out each piece into a 20 cm (8 inch) circle. Do not worry if the edges are a little uneven, it just adds to the rugged effect.

Dampen the edges with a little milk. Place a portion of the meat filling on half of each circle, fold over the pastry to cover and press the edges together to seal. Roll the pasties over so the edges are on the top and crimp with your fingers to form the traditional wavy pattern. Place on the baking tray, brush with the beaten egg and make two slits near the top of each side to allow steam to escape.

Bake in the middle of the oven for 10 minutes before reducing the heat to 180°C/350°F/ Gas Mark 4 for a further 30 minutes, or until the pasties are golden and the filling cooked.

Lamb & apple burger

Cook these on the barbecue and serve with salad leaves and tomato slices. Or grill them and serve with potato wedges and a spicy tomato relish.

Makes 6–8
Preparation and
 cooking time:
 25 minutes

450 g (1 lb) lean **lamb mince**
1 small **onion**, grated
1 small **eating apple**,
 peeled, cored and grated
1 teaspoon **ground cumin**
1 **chilli**, de-seeded and
 finely chopped
1 **egg**, beaten
50 g (1¾ oz) fresh
 wholemeal breadcrumbs
salt and freshly ground
 black pepper
1 tablespoon **sunflower oil**

To serve
1 **ciabatta bread**, sliced
1 **Little Gem lettuce**, torn
4 **tomatoes**, sliced
tomato chutney

Place the mince in a mixing bowl and add the onion, apple, cumin, chilli, egg, breadcrumbs and seasoning. Mix thoroughly. Shape the mixture into 6–8 even-sized burgers.

Brush both sides of the burgers with the oil and cook on a preheated grill or barbecue for 5–7 minutes, on each side, until cooked right through.

Serve between slices of the ciabatta bread, together with the lettuce, tomatoes and tomato chutney.

Main
meals

Tagliatelle bolognese

A classic Italian dish that is popular worldwide. This version includes white wine to produce a light sauce that is really delicious.

Serves 4
Preparation time:
  25 minutes
Cooking time:
  30–40 minutes

15 g (½ oz) **butter**
50 g (1¾ oz) lean **back bacon**, chopped
2 **garlic cloves**, finely chopped
1 large **onion**, finely chopped
2 **carrots**, peeled and diced
2 **celery sticks**, chopped
500 g (1 lb 2 oz) lean **beef mince**
400g can **chopped tomatoes**
3 tablespoons **tomato purée**
1 teaspoon **dried oregano**
150 ml (5 fl oz) **dry white wine**
150 ml (5 fl oz) **beef stock**
salt and freshly ground **black pepper**
225 g (8 oz) **tagliatelle**
grated **Parmesan cheese**, to serve

Melt the butter in a deep frying pan, add the bacon and fry for 2–3 minutes. Add the garlic, onion, carrots and celery and fry for 5 minutes until lightly browned. Add the mince and brown lightly.

Stir in the tomatoes, tomato purée, oregano, wine and stock, season and bring to the boil. Lower the heat and simmer for 30–40 minutes until the sauce is reduced and thick.

Meanwhile, bring a saucepan of water to the boil and cook the tagliatelle according to the packet instructions until just al dente.

Drain the tagliatelle and toss with the meat sauce. Sprinkle with grated Parmesan cheese to serve.

Spaghetti carbonara

This is a dream to make; you can rustle it up in next to no time. It also has the added bonus of being healthier than ready-made versions.

Serves 4
Preparation time:
 10 minutes
Cooking time:
 10 minutes

350 g (12 oz) **spaghetti**
1 tablespoon **olive oil**
175 g (6 oz) lean **back bacon**, snipped into pieces
3 **eggs**, lightly beaten
4 tablespoons grated **Parmesan cheese**
4 tablespoons **fromage frais**
freshly ground **black pepper**

To serve
1 tablespoon chopped fresh **parsley**
shaved **Parmesan cheese**

Bring a large saucepan of water to the boil and cook the spaghetti according to the packet instructions until just al dente.

Meanwhile, heat the oil in a frying pan. Add the bacon and fry over a high heat for about 5 minutes, until crisp and golden.

Beat together the eggs, Parmesan and fromage frais. Season with pepper to taste. Drain the pasta well and return it to the saucepan, away from direct heat.

Discard all but 1 tablespoon of fat from the bacon. Add this, plus the bacon, to the spaghetti, making sure that you scrape in any tasty, crunchy bits stuck to the bottom of the frying pan.

Pour in the egg mixture and mix everything together. Keep stirring until the spaghetti is thoroughly coated and the sauce is creamy and smooth. Serve at once, sprinkled with the parsley, Parmesan and a grinding of black pepper.

Tip Don't be tempted to return the pan to the hob after you have added the sauce – the eggs will scramble; just allow the heat of the pasta to cook the sauce through.

Tomato & basil conchiglie

This pasta dish has a very light and fresh taste. Do not boil the tomato sauce – this will keep the basil as green and as flavourful as possible.

Serves 4
Preparation time:
  10 minutes
Cooking time:
  20 minutes

350 g (12 oz) **pasta shells**
  (conchiglie)
4 **plum tomatoes**, skinned
  (see Tip)
25 g (1 oz) fresh **basil**,
  leaves removed from
  the stalks
4 tablespoons good **olive**
  oil, plus extra to serve
salt and freshly ground
  black pepper

To serve
tiny fresh **basil leaves**
shaved **Parmesan cheese**

Bring a large saucepan of water to the boil and cook the conchiglie according to the packet instructions until just al dente.

Meanwhile, roughly chop the tomatoes, saving all the juices, and put in a bowl. Lightly shred the basil leaves and add to the tomatoes with the oil. Season.

When the pasta is cooked, drain well, reserving 150 ml (5 fl oz) of the cooking liquid. Return the liquid to the saucepan, add the tomato mixture, and reheat without boiling.

Add the drained pasta, check the seasoning and quickly stir to mix. Divide between four pasta dishes and serve garnished with the basil, shaved Parmesan, a grinding of black pepper and a drizzle of olive oil.

Tip To skin the tomatoes, put them in a bowl, pour over boiling water, leave for 1 minute and then drain off the water. You will now be able to remove the skins easily. Use a sharp pointed knife to remove the core where the stalk was attached.

Mushroom tagliatelle

Wild mushrooms have a lot more flavour than regular mushrooms, but if you can't find them, any other mushrooms will do.

Serves 4
Preparation time:
   10 minutes
Cooking time:
   15 minutes

350 g (12 oz) **tagliatelle**
4 tablespoons **olive oil**
2 fat **garlic cloves**, thinly sliced
175 g (6 oz) **wild mushrooms**, roughly chopped
salt and freshly ground **black pepper**
2 tablespoons chopped fresh **parsley**

Bring a large saucepan of water to the boil and cook the tagliatelle according to the packet instructions until just al dente

Meanwhile, heat the oil in a small saucepan and fry the garlic slices until just beginning to brown.

Add the mushrooms to the garlic and cook for 4–5 minutes until the mushrooms soften and release their juices. Season.

Drain the pasta, return to the saucepan and pour over the mushroom mixture. Stir to mix and sprinkle in the parsley. Serve immediately.

Macaroni cheese

A classic family favourite, this ever-popular dish is always a hit with children and adults alike. Serve simply with a green salad.

Serves 3–4
Preparation time:
  20 minutes
Cooking time:
  15 minutes

225 g (8 oz) quick-cook
  macaroni

Cheese sauce
40 g (1½ oz) **butter**
40 g (1½ oz) **plain flour**
600 ml (20 fl oz)
  semi-skimmed milk
salt, **cayenne pepper** and
  mustard powder, to taste
175 g (6 oz) **Cheddar
  cheese**, grated
50 g (1¾ oz) **wholemeal
  breadcrumbs**

Bring a large saucepan of water to the boil and cook the macaroni according to the packet instructions until just al dente. Drain well.

For the cheese sauce, melt the butter in a saucepan. Add the flour and cook for 1 minute, stirring continuously with a wooden spoon. Remove the pan from the heat and gradually stir in the milk.

Return the pan to the heat and bring to the boil, stirring continuously to avoid lumps. Cook the sauce for 1 minute, still stirring continuously. Remove from the heat and add salt, cayenne pepper and mustard powder to taste. Add half the cheese and stir until it has melted. Preheat the grill to medium-high.

Mix the macaroni and cheese sauce together and place in a 1.7 litre (3 pint) pie dish. Mix together the remaining cheese and the breadcrumbs and sprinkle evenly over the top.

Toast under the grill until golden brown and serve immediately.

Ham & tomato pasta bake

This is ideal for using up any ham left over at Christmas time. Serve with a selection of lightly cooked green vegetables or a crisp green salad.

Serves 4
Preparation time:
  20 minutes
Cooking time:
  25–30 minutes

175 g (6 oz) **fusilli**
1 tablespoon **vegetable oil**
1 **onion**, chopped
2 **garlic cloves**, chopped
200 g (7 oz) **cooked ham**, cubed
400 g can **chopped tomatoes**
1 teaspoon **dried basil**
300 ml (10 fl oz) **semi-skimmed milk**
2 **eggs**
1 tablespoon **tomato purée**
freshly ground **black pepper**
75 g (2¾ oz) **mature Cheddar cheese**, grated

Preheat the oven to 180°C/350°F/Gas Mark 4.

Bring a large saucepan of water to the boil and cook the fusilli according to the packet instructions until just al dente. Drain thoroughly.

Meanwhile, heat the oil in a large frying pan and fry the onion and garlic for 5 minutes to soften. Add the ham, tomatoes and basil and simmer for 8–10 minutes.

Stir the cooked pasta gently into the ham and tomato mixture and stir gently to combine. Turn the mixture into a shallow ovenproof dish.

Whisk together the milk, eggs and tomato purée and season with black pepper. Pour the egg mixture over the pasta and sprinkle the grated Cheddar cheese over the top.

Bake for 25–30 minutes until the mixture is set and the top is golden brown. Serve immediately.

Beef olives

A time-honoured dish of slices of beef rolled around a simple vegetable stuffing. Serve with baby new potatoes and mixed roasted vegetables.

Serves 4
Preparation time:
 20 minutes
Cooking time:
 1½–2 hours

450 g (1 lb) **topside of beef**
salt and freshly ground
 black pepper
2 teaspoons **cornflour**
2 small **carrots**, peeled
 and finely diced
1 small **onion**, finely diced
1 teaspoon **dried mixed
 herbs**
1 tablespoon **tomato purée**
1 tablespoon
 Worcestershire sauce
150 ml (5 fl oz) **beef stock**
150 ml (5 fl oz) **red wine**
4 rashers **unsmoked streaky
 bacon**
1 tablespoon finely chopped
 fresh **parsley**, to garnish
 (optional)

Preheat the oven to 180°C/350°F/Gas Mark 4. Carve the topside into four thick slices. Place each slice between sheets of greaseproof paper and flatten them by bashing with a rolling pin or meat hammer. Season.

Blend the cornflour with a little cold water to make a paste. In a bowl, mix together the carrots, onion, herbs, tomato purée, Worcestershire sauce, blended cornflour and 4 tablespoons of the stock.

Divide the stuffing mixture between the flattened slices and roll up each into a neat parcel. Wrap each parcel with a rasher of bacon and tie securely with string.

Place the parcels in a shallow roasting tin or ovenproof baking dish and pour in the remaining stock and the red wine. Cover the dish tightly with foil and cook for 1½–2 hours or until the meat is really tender.

To serve, remove the string from each parcel and garnish with the parsley, if using. These aer delicious served with ratatouille.

Tip Ask your butcher to cut four slices of topside for you, rather than buying one big piece.

Moussaka

Make this ahead and then cook for when your friends arrive; all it needs is a crisp salad of mixed leaves to accompany.

Serves 4
Preparation and
cooking time: 2 hours

450 g (1 lb) **aubergines**
sea salt
450 g (1 lb) lean **lamb mince**
1 large **onion**, finely
   chopped
1 tablespoon **plain flour**
400 g can **chopped tomatoes**
1 fat **garlic clove**, crushed
2 teaspoons **tomato purée**
1 tablespoon chopped fresh
   parsley
1 teaspoon **ground**
   cinnamon
½ teaspoon **dried oregano**
1 **bay leaf**
freshly ground **black pepper**
2–3 tablespoons **olive oil**
450 g (1 lb) **cooked waxy**
   potatoes, sliced

Topping
300 g (10½ oz) **Greek yogurt**
2 **eggs**, beaten
50 g (1¾ oz) **Parmesan**
   cheese, finely grated
a little freshly grated **nutmeg**

Remove the stalks from the aubergines and cut into 1 cm (½ inch) slices. Layer in a colander, sprinkling a little salt between each layer. Weigh down and leave for 30 minutes to extract any bitter juices.

Meanwhile, brown the mince and onion in a non-stick lidded saucepan over a high heat, breaking up any lumps. Reduce the heat, stir in the flour and cook for 1 minute. Add the tomatoes, garlic, tomato purée, parsley, cinnamon, oregano and bay leaf. Season, bring to the boil, cover the pan, reduce the heat and simmer for 30 minutes, stirring occasionally. Preheat the grill to high.

Rinse the salt from the aubergines and pat them dry with a tea towel. Arrange in a single layer on the grill pan and brush with half the olive oil. Grill for about 5 minutes, or until golden. Turn, brush with the remaining oil and grill again until golden.

Preheat the oven to 180°C/350°F/Gas Mark 4 and lightly grease a 2.3 litre (4 pint) ovenproof dish.

Remove the bay leaf from the mince and adjust the seasoning if necessary. Arrange half the aubergine slices over the base of the dish, and half the potato slices on top of them. Pour the lamb sauce over the top. Finish with the remaining aubergine and potato slices.

In a bowl, whisk together the yogurt, eggs and Parmesan. Season and pour over the potato, covering it completely. Sprinkle a little grated nutmeg over the top and bake for about 40 minutes, until puffy and golden.

Chicken korma

Serves 4
Preparation and
cooking time:
1 hour 10 minutes

4 tablespoons **sunflower oil**
3 **onions**
3 **garlic cloves**, crushed
2 teaspoons grated fresh
   root ginger
1 tablespoon **ground**
   coriander
1½ teaspoons **ground cumin**
1 **cinnamon stick**, halved
½ teaspoon **turmeric**
10 **green cardamom pods**,
   seeds removed and
   ground
4 **cloves**, ground or a pinch
   of **ground cloves**
2 **bay leaves**
4 skinless, boneless
   chicken breasts, each cut
   into 8 chunks
50 g (1¾ oz) **flaked almonds**
425 g (15 oz) **Greek yogurt**
2 teaspoons **cornflour**
sea salt and freshly ground
   black pepper
a squeeze of **lemon juice**
fresh **coriander leaves**, to
   garnish

Heat 2 tablespoons of oil in a lidded wok or large lidded frying pan. Thinly slice one of the onions and fry for about 10 minutes, until crisp and brown. Remove with a slotted spoon and drain on kitchen towel. Keep warm.

Heat the remaining oil in the same wok or pan. Finely chop the remaining onions. Fry with the garlic and ginger for about 10 minutes, until soft and golden. Reduce the heat, add the spices and bay leaves and cook for a couple of minutes. Stir in the chicken and almonds and blend in 150 ml (5 fl oz) of cold water.

Combine the yogurt and cornflour (this helps to prevent the sauce from curdling) and gradually stir into the chicken mixture. Season. Bring to a simmer, cover and cook for 15–20 minutes, stirring occasionally.

Remove the cinnamon stick and bay leaves. Squeeze in a little lemon juice and adjust the seasoning to taste. Serve topped with the browned onion rings and scattered with coriander leaves.

To make pilau rice for the perfect accompaniment, first rinse 225 g (8 oz) of jasmine or basmati rice well. Sauté in a little oil with some chopped onion before cooking it in 350 ml (12 fl oz) of boiling stock, with ½ teaspoon of turmeric, a handful of sultanas, a few cardamom pods, a cinnamon stick and a bay leaf.

Spicy beef stir fry

Always prepare the ingredients before starting to cook a stir fry to ensure that cooking flows as rapidly as possible. Serve with cooked noodles or rice.

Serves 4
**Preparation and
  cooking time:
  35 minutes**

350 g (12 oz) lean **rump
  steak**, finely sliced
1½ teaspoons **Chinese five
  spice**
2 teaspoons **cornflour**
1 tablespoon **vegetable oil**
1 **onion**, sliced
1 **garlic clove**, finely
  chopped
1 **red chilli**, de-seeded and
  finely chopped
4 cm (1½ inches) fresh **root
  ginger**, finely chopped
1 **red pepper**, de-seeded
  and sliced
1 **green pepper**, de-seeded
  and sliced
125 g (4½ oz) **baby corn**,
  sliced on the diagonal
150 ml (5 fl oz) **beef stock**
3 tablespoons **oyster sauce**
freshly ground **black pepper**
3 **spring onions**, finely
  sliced, to garnish

Toss the steak with the Chinese five spice and cornflour to coat the meat. Set aside.

Heat the oil in a wok or large frying pan and stir fry the onion slices for 2 minutes. Add the garlic, chilli and ginger and fry for a further minute. Finally, add the peppers and baby corn and stir fry until the vegetables are just tender – no more than 3–4 minutes. Transfer the vegetables to a plate and keep warm.

Add the beef to the wok or pan and stir fry to brown completely. Pour in the stock and oyster sauce and cook for about 2 minutes until the stock thickens slightly. Season with black pepper.

Return the vegetables to the wok and stir fry for a further 2 minutes until everything is heated through. Take care not to overcook. Serve immediately, sprinkled with the sliced spring onions.

Turkey & leek pie

Instead of brushing the filo pastry with melted butter, use it as it is. The pastry will still bake to an attractive golden colour.

Serves 6
Preparation time:
40 minutes
Cooking time:
20–30 minutes

2 tablespoons **vegetable oil**
750 g (1 lb 10 oz) skinless,
  boneless **turkey breast**,
  cubed
2 **leeks**, sliced
2 **celery sticks**, sliced
1 **onion**, sliced
2 small **carrots**, peeled
  and sliced
2 tablespoons **plain flour**
150 ml (5 fl oz) **dry cider**
300 ml (10 fl oz) **chicken
  stock**
1 tablespoon **Dijon mustard**
2 tablespoons **crème
  fraîche**
freshly ground **black pepper**
6 sheets **filo pastry**
1 teaspoon **sesame seeds**

Preheat the oven to 200ºC/400°F/Gas Mark 6.

Heat 1 tablespoon of the oil in a large lidded saucepan and fry the turkey in batches until golden brown. Set aside. Add the vegetables to the pan and gently sauté for 4–5 minutes. Sprinkle over the flour and cook for 1 minute.

Gradually stir in the cider and stock, followed by the mustard, and bring up to the boil, stirring to allow the sauce to thicken. Return the turkey to the pan. Reduce the heat, cover the pan and simmer gently for 15–20 minutes until the vegetables are tender. Stir in the crème fraîche and season with black pepper. Transfer the mixture to a shallow ovenproof dish.

Take one sheet of filo pastry at a time, spread it out on a clean work surface and lightly brush with the remaining oil. Crumple each sheet slightly and arrange on top of the turkey mixture to cover it completely. Sprinkle over the sesame seeds.

Bake the pie for 20–30 minutes until the pastry is cooked through and the filling is piping hot. Cover the top with foil if the pastry appears to be browning too quickly. Serve immediately.

Steak, kidney & whisky pie

A traditional comfort food, but with a modern twist – steak, kidney and onions flavoured with whisky and topped with puff pastry.

Serves 4
Preparation time:
  2 hours 30 minutes
Cooking time:
  30–40 minutes

2 tablespoons **plain flour**
salt and freshly ground
  black pepper
675 g (1 lb 8 oz) **braising
  steak**, diced
225 g (8 oz) **lamb's kidneys**,
  chopped
2 tablespoons **vegetable oil**
1 large **onion**, thinly sliced
4 tablespoons **whisky**
425 ml (15 fl oz) **beef stock**
350 g (12 oz) ready-made
  puff pastry
beaten **egg**, to glaze

Mix together the flour and seasoning on a plate. Coat the steak and kidneys evenly in the seasoned flour.

Heat the oil in a large lidded saucepan and fry the meat for 5–6 minutes until browned all over. Transfer to a plate.

Add the onion to the pan and fry until soft. Stir in the whisky and simmer until all the liquid has evaporated.

Return the meat and juices to the pan and gradually stir in the stock. Season. Cover and simmer gently for 2 hours or until the beef is tender. Leave to cool. Preheat the oven to 200°C/400°F/Gas Mark 6.

Spoon the cooled mixture into a 1 litre (1¾ pint) pie dish. Roll out the pastry 2.5 cm (1 inch) wider than the dish. Cut out a wide strip of pastry to fit the edge of the dish and stick it to the rim with water. Place the pastry lid on the dish and trim if necessary. Crimp the edges. Cut out leaf shapes from any remaining pastry and stick in place with water. Brush with beaten egg and make a slit in the top.

Bake for 30–40 minutes until the pastry is risen and golden.

Shepherd's pie

Traditionally, shepherd's pie is made from lamb and cottage pie from beef. Adding 'hidden' vegetables is an easy way of boosting your 5-a-day.

Serves 4
Preparation and
cooking time:
  1 hour 30 minutes

450 g (1 lb) **minced lamb**
1 large **onion**, chopped
1 tablespoon **plain flour**
300 ml (10 fl oz) good **lamb**
  stock
115 g (4 oz) **button**
  mushrooms, finely sliced
1 tablespoon
  Worcestershire sauce
1 tablespoon **tomato purée**
2 tablespoons chopped
  fresh **parsley**
1 **bay leaf**
freshly ground **black pepper**

Potato & leek topping
700 g (1 lb 9 oz) **potatoes**,
  peeled and quartered
25 g (1 oz) **butter**
2 **leeks**, very finely sliced
3 tablespoons **milk**
80 g (3 oz) **Cheddar cheese**,
  grated

Brown the mince and onion in a large, lidded, non-stick pan over a high heat, breaking up any lumps of meat. Reduce the heat and stir in the flour. Cook through for 1 minute.

Gradually blend in the stock. Add the mushrooms, Worcestershire sauce, tomato purée, parsley and bay leaf and season to taste with pepper. Bring to the boil, cover, reduce the heat and simmer for 30 minutes, until the lamb is cooked. Stir occasionally.

Meanwhile, bring a saucepan of water to the boil, add the potatoes, cover and simmer for 15–20 minutes, or until cooked.

While the potatoes are cooking, melt the butter in a frying pan and sauté the leeks over a low heat for 10 minutes until softened, but not brown.

Preheat the oven to 200°C/400°F/Gas Mark 6. Grease a 2 litre (3½ pint) ovenproof dish.

Drain the potatoes and return to the heat to dry off any excess moisture. Mash until lump free. Beat in the leeks, milk and 50 g (1¾ oz) of the cheese. Adjust the seasoning to taste.

Remove the bay leaf from the mince. Add a little extra stock if the mixture seems dry and then pour into the prepared dish. Spoon the potato over the top and roughly smooth the surface. Sprinkle with the remaining grated cheese and bake for 30 minutes, until the top is crisp and golden. Alternatively brown under a hot grill, whichever is more convenient.

Tips If making in advance and cooking the pie straight from the fridge, it will take about 45 minutes to heat through thoroughly.

Try making this in four individual pie dishes for perfect little servings.

Fish pie

Serves **4**
Preparation time:
  40 minutes
Cooking time:
  45 minutes

450 g (1 lb) **white fish fillets**,
  skinned and cut into
  2.5 cm (1 inch) cubes
115 g (4½ oz) **cooked
  shelled prawns**
2 **hard-boiled eggs**,
  quartered

Potato topping
675 g (1 lb 8 oz) **potatoes**,
  peeled and quartered
3 tablespoons **milk**
25 g (1 oz) **butter**
sea salt and freshly ground
  black pepper

Parsley sauce
40 g (1½ oz) **butter**
40 g (1½ oz) **plain flour**
425 ml (15 fl oz) **milk**,
  warmed
a squeeze of **lemon juice**
1 tablespoon chopped fresh
  parsley
freshly ground **black pepper**

Preheat the oven to 200°C/400°F/Gas Mark 6 and place a baking tray on a high shelf. Grease a 2 litre (3½ pint) shallow ovenproof dish.

Place the potatoes in a large lidded saucepan, cover with cold water, bring to the boil, cover and simmer for about 15–20 minutes, or until they are cooked.

Meanwhile, make the parsley sauce. Melt the butter, stir in the flour and cook for 1 minute. Gradually blend in the milk, bring to the boil and simmer for a couple of minutes. Stir in the lemon juice and parsley and season to taste with black pepper.

Arrange the fish in a single layer over the base of the prepared dish. Scatter over the prawns and place the hard-boiled eggs on top. Pour over the parsley sauce, covering the fish completely.

Drain the potatoes and return to the heat to dry off any excess moisture. Mash until lump free and then beat in the milk and butter. Season to taste.

Spoon the mash equally over the fish and sauce. Smooth the top and then fork through a pattern. Bake for 45 minutes, until the fish is cooked and the potato golden.

Tip Including some cooked spinach in the base could make a dinner party variation of this pie. Use a mixture of white wine and stock instead of milk for the sauce, and slices of cooked potato for the topping.

Baked lemon trout

This is a straightforward but delicious way of cooking trout. It only needs a simple accompaniment of new potatoes and steamed mange tout.

Serves 4
Preparation time:
  20 minutes
Cooking time:
  25 minutes

2 tablespoons **olive oil**, plus
  extra for greasing
4 **whole trout**
freshly ground **black pepper**

Stuffing
125 g (4½ oz) fresh **white**
  breadcrumbs
2 tablespoons chopped
  fresh **parsley**
2 **garlic cloves**, finely
  chopped
grated zest and juice of
  2 **lemons**
4 tablespoons **olive oil**

Preheat the oven to 190°C/375°F/Gas Mark 5. Lightly grease a roasting tin large enough to hold the four trout.

To prepare the stuffing, place the breadcrumbs, parsley, garlic and lemon zest in a bowl. Stir in the olive oil and 1 tablespoon of lemon juice. Season with black pepper and mix well to combine the ingredients.

Divide the stuffing evenly between the cavities of the four trout. Place the trout side by side in the roasting tin.

In a small bowl, whisk together the 2 tablespoons of olive oil and a further tablespoon of lemon juice. Season lightly with black pepper and drizzle the dressing over the trout.

Bake for 20–25 minutes or until the fish is cooked. Serve immediately, spooning any pan juices over the trout.

Tomato crusted salmon

Use sunblush or semi-cuit tomatoes for this recipe in preference to sun-dried tomatoes, because they are brighter in colour and more moist.

Serves 4
Preparation time:
 20 minutes
Cooking time:
 15–20 minutes

4 × 150–175 g (5½–6 oz) skinless **salmon fillets**
75 g (2¾ oz) fresh **white breadcrumbs**
finely grated zest of ½ a **lemon**
25 g (1 oz) stoned **black olives**, finely chopped
25 g (1 oz) **sunblush tomatoes**, finely chopped
1 tablespoon finely chopped fresh **flat leaf parsley**
2 tablespoons **olive oil**

Roasted tomatoes
1 packet **cherry tomatoes** on the vine
1 tablespoon **olive oil**
freshly ground **black pepper**

Preheat the oven to 200ºC/400°F/Gas Mark 6. Line a baking tray with non-stick baking parchment and place the salmon fillets on it.

In a small bowl, mix together the breadcrumbs, lemon zest, olives, sunblush tomatoes and parsley. Add the olive oil and stir well to moisten the breadcrumbs and combine the ingredients.

Spoon the breadcrumb mixture evenly over the salmon pieces and press it down lightly to form a crust. Bake in the oven for 15–20 minutes until the salmon is cooked and the breadcrumbs are lightly golden and crusty.

Meanwhile, place the cherry tomatoes, still on their stalks, in a small roasting tin. Drizzle over the olive oil and add a grinding of black pepper. Bake in the oven for 10–15 minutes along with the fish until just tender and softened.

To serve, place a salmon portion on a warmed plate and top each one with a few of the tomatoes still on their vine.

Hake baked en papillote

This is a really good way of cooking fish: the sealed 'packets' keep in the flavours and save on the washing up.

Serves 4
**Preparation and
  cooking time:
  20 minutes**

1 **lemon**
4 × 175 g (6 oz) skinned **hake**
  or **haddock fillets**
12 stoned **black olives**,
  roughly chopped
freshly ground **black pepper**
a little **olive oil**
4 **bay leaves** (optional)

Preheat the oven to 190°C/375°F/Gas Mark 5. Prepare four large pieces of non-stick baking parchment, each folded in half. Grate the zest from the lemon and then thinly slice the fruit.

Lay each piece of fish on a piece of baking parchment and top each with two lemon slices. Add a bay leaf, if using. Sprinkle over a portion of the olives and lemon zest and season with black pepper. Finish by drizzling a little olive oil over each piece of fish.

Fold the paper around the fish, folding the edges a couple of times to keep the juices in, and then tie each parcel with string. Put on a flat baking tray and bake for 15 minutes.

Serve the wrapped parcels as they are – open them up on your plate and let the juices run out.

Tip You can substitute sliced tomatoes, chopped coriander or a little garlic for the olives – experiment as much as you want.

Broccoli & salmon roulade

Savoury roulades make an excellent main course for a warm summer day or, sliced thinly, a very acceptable starter.

Serves 4–6
Preparation and
cooking time:
 50 minutes + 1 hour
 chilling

225 g (8 oz) **broccoli florets**
4 **eggs**, separated
a generous pinch of grated
 nutmeg
freshly ground **black pepper**
15 g (½ oz) **Cheddar cheese**,
 grated

Filling
200 g (7 oz) **smoked salmon**
 slices
200 g (7 oz) **cream cheese**
2 tablespoons **low fat**
 natural yogurt
2 ripe **tomatoes**, peeled,
 de-seeded and finely
 chopped
1 tablespoon snipped fresh
 chives

Preheat the oven to 220ºC/425°F/Gas Mark 7. Line a 33 × 23 cm (13 × 9 inch) Swiss roll tin with non-stick baking parchment.

Steam or gently simmer the broccoli florets until tender. Drain thoroughly, turn them out on to a plate and chop finely. Place in a large bowl with the egg yolks, nutmeg and a grinding of black pepper. Mix well.

In a separate large clean bowl, whisk the egg whites until stiff but not dry. Stir 1 tablespoon of egg white into the broccoli mixture to loosen it slightly, and then carefully fold in the remainder, taking care not to knock out any of the volume. Spread the broccoli mixture evenly into the prepared tin and bake for 10–12 minutes until firm and lightly golden.

Place a clean sheet of non-stick baking parchment on the work surface and sprinkle over the grated Cheddar. Turn the roulade out on to the paper and leave to cool for 5 minutes. Peel off the lining paper.

Carefully separate the slices of smoked salmon and lay them over the surface of the roulade. Mix together the cream cheese, yogurt, tomatoes and chives and spread in an even layer over the smoked salmon.

Using the sheet of baking parchment, roll up the roulade in the same way as a Swiss roll and, leaving it in the paper, chill in the fridge for about 1 hour to firm up. When ready to serve, remove the roulade from the paper and cut into thick slices.

Tomato & spinach lasagne

Tomato, spinach and ricotta are classic flavourings for pasta. Any left over can be frozen and used another time. Serve with a salad.

Serves 4–6
Preparation and cooking time: 70–75 minutes

8 **lasagne sheets**
25 g (1 oz) **Cheddar cheese**, grated
1 tablespoon grated **Parmesan cheese**
torn fresh **basil**, to garnish

Tomato sauce
1 tablespoon **olive oil**
1 **onion**, finely chopped
2 **garlic cloves**, crushed
2 × 400 g cans **chopped tomatoes**
1 tablespoon **tomato purée**
½ teaspoon **dried basil**
½ teaspoon **caster sugar**
150 ml (5 fl oz) **vegetable stock**

Spinach layer
450 g (1 lb) **frozen spinach**, defrosted
250 g (9 oz) **ricotta cheese**
½ teaspoon **ground nutmeg**
freshly ground **black pepper**

Preheat the oven to 190ºC/375°F/Gas Mark 5.

To make the tomato sauce, heat the olive oil in a large lidded saucepan and gently cook the onion and garlic until softened. Add the tomatoes, tomato purée, basil, sugar and stock. Bring up to the boil, cover and then reduce the heat and simmer for 20–25 minutes until the sauce has slightly thickened.

Meanwhile, place the spinach in a sieve and, using the back of a wooden spoon, press against it to remove as much of the excess water as possible. Turn the spinach into a bowl and mix in the ricotta, nutmeg and a good grinding of black pepper.

Pour half the tomato sauce over the base of a shallow 20 × 28 cm (8 × 11 inch) ovenproof dish. Layer four lasagne sheets over the sauce. Spread over the spinach and ricotta mixture, and then layer with the last four lasagne sheets. Cover with the remaining tomato sauce. Sprinkle over the Cheddar cheese and grated Parmesan.

Bake for 25–30 minutes until the cheese on top is melted and lightly browned and the lasagne is heated through. Serve immediately, garnished with the torn basil.

Carrot & chestnut filo pie

Crisp filo pastry contrasts well with the soft filling in this pie recipe. Serve hot, accompanied by boiled new potatoes and lightly steamed broccoli.

Serves 6
Preparation time:
40 minutes
Cooking time:
30 minutes

3 tablespoons **olive oil**
1 large **onion**, chopped
2 **garlic cloves**, chopped
600 g (1 lb 5 oz) **carrots**, peeled and grated
½ teaspoon **dried marjoram**
250 g (9 oz) **chestnut mushrooms**, sliced
200 g (7 oz) **peeled cooked chestnuts**, roughly chopped
200 g (7 oz) **cashew nuts**, roughly chopped
3 tablespoons chopped fresh **flat leaf parsley**
3 tablespoons **tomato purée**
200 g (7 oz) **cream cheese**
freshly ground **black pepper**
6 large **filo pastry sheets**
a little **milk**, for glazing

Preheat the oven to 180°C/350°F/Gas Mark 4. Place a circle of non-stick baking parchment in the base of a deep, round, 20–23 cm (8–9 inch) springform baking tin.

Heat 2 tablespoons of the olive oil in a large lidded saucepan. Gently fry the onion and garlic for 4–5 minutes to soften. Add the carrots and marjoram, reduce the heat, cover the pan and sweat the vegetables for 10 minutes, stirring occasionally. Remove from the heat and set aside to cool slightly.

Meanwhile, heat the remaining tablespoon of oil in a separate pan and sauté the mushrooms for 3–4 minutes. Add the chestnuts, cashew nuts, parsley and tomato purée along with 2 tablespoons of water. Simmer for a further 2–3 minutes.

Stir the cream cheese into the cooled carrots, and then combine the carrot mixture with the mushrooms. Season with plenty of black pepper.

Working quickly so that the filo pastry doesn't dry out, arrange four overlapping sheets of pastry across the base of the prepared tin, easing it into the sides and up over the edge of the tin. Spoon the carrot and nut mixture into the tin and level the top. Cover with the fifth sheet of filo pastry, folding as necessary, and then turn down the overhanging pieces of filo. Lightly scrunch up the last sheet of pastry and arrange it attractively over the top of the pie. Brush with a little milk to glaze.

Bake for 30 minutes until the pastry is crisp and golden. Leave to rest for a couple of minutes before removing from the tin and serving.

Tomato tarte tatin

This is a savoury tarte tatin – really an upside down tomato pie. With good-flavoured tomatoes, it makes an unusual supper or light lunch dish.

Serves 6
Preparation time:
 20 minutes
Cooking time:
 30 minutes

225 g (8 oz) **plain flour**
1 heaped teaspoon **baking powder**
salt and freshly ground **black pepper**
50 g (1¾ oz) **butter**, cubed
150 ml (5 fl oz) **semi-skimmed milk**
2 tablespoons **olive oil**
700 g (1 lb 9 oz) **heritage tomatoes**, halved or quartered if large, or other good-flavoured **vine tomatoes**
1 teaspoon chopped fresh **basil**, plus 8 fresh **basil leaves**, torn, to garnish
2 teaspoons **balsamic vinegar**

Sieve the flour and baking powder into a large bowl and season. Rub in the butter using just your fingertips. Add the milk to make a soft dough and set aside. Preheat the oven to 220°C/425°F/Gas Mark 7.

Pour the oil into a shallow, 24 cm (9½ inch) round ovenproof dish. Lay the tomatoes on the bottom of the dish, sprinkle over the chopped basil and balsamic vinegar and season.

Roll the dough out to fit over the tomatoes, put it over the top of them and tuck the edges inside the dish to seal. Cook in the oven for about 30 minutes until the crust is well risen and golden.

Remove from the oven and release the edges with a knife. Leave to cool for 4 minutes and then turn upside down on to a serving dish. Scatter over the fresh basil and serve warm.

Chick pea burgers & salsa

These spicy burgers make a great alternative to meat. They can also be served in a wholemeal bun with red onion slices and salad.

Serves 4
**Preparation and
    cooking time:
    40 minutes + at least
    1 hour cooling**

2 × 400 g cans **chick peas**,
    drained and rinsed
2 tablespoons **olive oil**
1 small **onion**, finely
    chopped
1 **garlic clove**, crushed
1 **red pepper**, de-seeded
    and finely chopped
2 tablespoons chopped
    fresh **coriander**
1 **red chilli**, de-seeded and
    finely chopped
salt and freshly ground
    black pepper
sunflower oil or **cooking
    spray**, for frying

Salsa
2 **tomatoes**, finely chopped
½ **red onion**, thinly sliced
1 tablespoon chopped fresh
    coriander
lime juice
olive oil

Put the chick peas into a food processor and pulse two or three times to lightly crush – you do not want them to be mushy but to retain some texture. Turn into a large bowl.

Heat the olive oil in a frying pan and gently fry the onion, garlic and pepper for 5 minutes to soften. Add to the chick peas with the coriander, chilli and seasoning.

Stir to mix well and chill in the fridge for at least 1 hour or overnight. Divide the mixture into eight and shape into burgers (you may need a little flour to do this).

Heat the sunflower oil or cooking spray in a non-stick frying pan and fry the burgers for 3 minutes on each side until they are golden and crispy. Drain on kitchen towel.

Mix all the salsa ingredients together, adding lime juice and a little olive oil to taste. Serve the burgers warm with the tomato salsa.

Desserts
& bakes

Bramley apple pie

This recipe contains 900 g (2 lb) of fruit, which makes a big dome under the pastry crust to begin with but subsides during cooking.

Serves 4–6
Preparation time:
  25 minutes +
  30 minutes chilling
Cooking time:
  40 minutes

Pastry
40 g (1½ oz) **unsalted butter**
  or **margarine**, cubed
40 g (1½ oz) **white**
  vegetable fat, cubed
175 g (6 oz) **plain flour**

Filling
50 g (1¾ oz) **caster sugar**,
  plus about 1 teaspoon
  for sprinkling
1 rounded tablespoon
  cornflour
900 g (2 lb) **Bramley apples**,
  peeled, cored and thinly
  sliced
1 tablespoon **elderflower**
  cordial (optional)
milk, for brushing

For the pastry, rub the butter or margarine and vegetable fat into the flour until the mixture resembles fine breadcrumbs. Sprinkle over 2 tablespoons of cold water and bring it all together to form a ball of dough. Knead very gently until just smooth. Wrap in cling film and chill for 30 minutes. Preheat the oven to 190°C/375°F/Gas Mark 5.

For the filling, mix together the sugar and cornflour. Using an 850 ml (1½ pint) pie dish, layer the sliced apples with the sugar and cornflour mixture, packing the fruit down well. Pour the elderflower cordial, if using, over the top.

On a lightly floured surface, roll out the pastry to 2.5 cm (1 inch) larger than the top of the pie dish. Cut off a 2.5 cm (1 inch) strip all around the outside of the pastry. Brush the rim of the pie dish with milk and then lightly press the strip of pastry on to it. Brush the pastry strip with some more milk and lift the remaining pastry on to it, to make a lid. Pinch the edges to seal and make a decorative pattern with thumb and forefingers, or a fork. Use any leftover pastry to make decorative hearts for the edge of the lid.

Brush the top of the pie with milk and sprinkle with a little caster sugar. Using a sharp knife, make a cross in the centre to allow steam to escape. Place on a baking tray and cook on a high shelf for about 40 minutes or until the pastry is golden and the apples are soft. Serve hot or cold.

Almond plum crumbles

There is something about cooked plums that results in a fabulous base for crumbles. The almonds add an extra special touch.

Serves 6
Preparation time:
  20 minutes
Cooking time:
  20–25 minutes

800 g (1 lb 11 oz) **plums**, quartered and stoned
75 g (2¾ oz) **golden granulated sugar**

Crumble
115 g (4¼ oz) **plain flour**
50 g (1¾ oz) **golden granulated sugar**
50 g (1¾ oz) **unsalted butter**, cubed
50 g (1¾ oz) **ground almonds**
25 g (1 oz) **flaked almonds**

Preheat the oven to 180°C/350°F/Gas Mark 4. Grease six individual pudding basins and place on a baking tray.

Place the plums in a large saucepan with the sugar and 3 tablespoons of water. Cook for 5 minutes until just beginning to soften.

Meanwhile, for the crumble, place the flour and sugar in a large bowl. Rub in the butter until the mixture resembles fine breadcrumbs. Stir in the ground almonds and half the flaked almonds.

Divide the plums between the pudding basins and scatter the crumble mixture over the tops. Press down lightly. Sprinkle the reserved flaked almonds over the tops.

Bake the crumbles in the centre of the oven for 20–25 minutes, until the crumble is golden and the juices are beginning to bubble up over the edges. Serve hot or warm.

Variation Rhubarb, with some ground ginger rubbed into the crumble topping, would make a delicious alternative.

Poached chocolate pears

I love this combination; the pears and chocolate sauce can be prepared in advance and simply assembled before serving.

Serves 6
Preparation time:
  10 minutes
Cooking time:
  15 minutes

6 ripe **pears**
2 tablespoons fresh **lemon juice**
80 g (3 oz) **caster sugar**
1 **cinnamon stick**

Chocolate sauce
225 g (8 oz) **plain chocolate** (at least 70% cocoa solids), broken into pieces
50 g (1¾ oz) **unsalted butter**, cubed
2 tablespoons **brandy**

Peel the pears, leaving the stalks intact. Scoop out the cores from the base and then brush the pears all over with lemon juice to prevent them from browning.

Place the sugar and 300 ml (10 fl oz) of water in a large lidded saucepan and heat gently until the sugar has dissolved. Add the pears and cinnamon stick, together with any remaining lemon juice, and top up with some more water if the pears are not completely covered. Bring to the boil, lower the heat, cover with a lid and simmer for about 15 minutes, until the pears are tender.

While the pears are cooking, make the chocolate sauce. Place the chocolate, butter and 175 ml (6 fl oz) of water in a saucepan and stir over a moderate heat until the chocolate and butter have melted. Whisk so that the sauce is smooth. Allow to cool a little and then stir in the brandy.

To serve, remove the pears from the syrup with a slotted spoon, transfer to a serving dish and keep warm. Boil the syrup over a high heat until it has reduced to 60 ml (2½ fl oz). Remove the cinnamon stick and stir it into the chocolate sauce. Serve the pears with the sauce.

Blackberry apple crumble

Few people can resist a hot fruit crumble and blackberries and apples are always a popular combination.

Serves 4–6
Preparation time:
  25 minutes
Cooking time:
  30–40 minutes

675 g (1½ lb) **Bramley apples**, peeled, cored and thinly sliced
225 g (8 oz) **blackberries**
4 tablespoons **granulated sugar**

Crumble
115 g (4¼ oz) **plain flour**
115 g (4¼ oz) **ground almonds**
80 g (3 oz) **caster sugar**
175 g (6 oz) **unsalted butter**, cubed
50 g (1¾ oz) **flaked almonds**

Preheat the oven to 180°C/350°F/Gas Mark 4. Place the apples and blackberries at the bottom of a 1.2 litre (2 pint) greased ovenproof dish and sprinkle the granulated sugar over.

Combine the flour, ground almonds and caster sugar in a large mixing bowl. Add the butter and rub into the flour mixture until it resembles breadcrumbs. Fold in half the flaked almonds and spoon the mixture over the fruit. Sprinkle the remaining flaked almonds on top.

Bake in the oven for 30–40 minutes, until the crumble is golden brown.

Serve hot with custard or single cream.

Poached plums

Victoria plums are the best, available from August to September, but other varieties are almost as good. This can be prepared the day before.

Serves 4
**Preparation and
   cooking time:
   1 hour + at least
   1 hour cooling**

1 wineglass fruity **red wine**
75 g (2¾ oz) **golden
   granulated sugar**
500 g (1 lb 2 oz) **plums**,
   stoned
50 g (1¾ oz) **flaked almonds**,
   lightly browned under the
   grill, to decorate

Add enough water to the wine to make it up to 600 ml (20 fl oz). Put the liquid and sugar into a large lidded saucepan, bring to the boil and simmer for 2 minutes until the sugar has dissolved.

Put in the plums one by one with a slotted spoon. They need to be in a single layer and completely covered with the liquid.

Bring back to the boil, cover and simmer for 3–4 minutes for Victoria plums and a little longer for larger, harder varieties. Turn off the heat and leave the plums in the juice (still covered) for 30 minutes.

Remove the plums with a slotted spoon. Boil the juice to reduce by half, pour over the plums and leave to cool for at least an hour, or preferably overnight.

Serve cold in a pretty glass bowl with the almonds sprinkled over at the last moment.

Elderflower peach cobbler

You don't often get cobblers these days, which is a shame as they are so delicious and satisfying. They also look impressive.

Serves 6
Preparation time:
  40 minutes
Cooking time:
  40 minutes

6 **peaches**, halved and
  stoned
115 g (4 oz) **caster sugar**,
  or to taste
a knob of **unsalted butter**
2–3 tablespoons
  elderflower cordial

Cobbler
225 g (8 oz) **self-raising flour**
a pinch of **salt**
100 g (3½ oz) **unsalted**
  butter, cubed
50 g (1¾ oz) **caster sugar**
1 large **egg**, beaten
4 tablespoons
  semi-skimmed milk, plus
  extra for brushing
golden granulated sugar,
  for sprinkling

Place the peaches, caster sugar and butter in a saucepan and cook over a very gentle heat until the butter has melted. Add the cordial and raise the heat a little. Bring to the boil and simmer for 1 minute. Transfer to a 1.2 litre (2 pint) greased, deep, ovenproof dish.

Preheat the oven to 200°C/400°F/Gas Mark 6.

To make the cobbler topping, sift the flour and salt into a large bowl, add the butter and rub in until the mixture resembles breadcrumbs. Stir in the sugar and add the egg and two-thirds of the milk. Bring the mixture together using a knife, adding a little more milk if needed.

Roll out the mixture on a lightly floured surface to 1 cm (½ inch) thick and cut into 4 cm (1½ inch) rounds. Arrange the scones on top of the peaches, brush with a little milk and sprinkle with the granulated sugar.

Bake for 10 minutes and then reduce the oven temperature to 180°C/350°F/Gas Mark 4. Continue to cook for another 25–30 minutes, until the scones are cooked and golden brown. Serve hot or warm, with custard or thick cream.

Baked stuffed apples

This is a traditional style dessert, but with a delicious stuffing. Serve with custard to pour over.

Serves 4
Preparation time:
20 minutes
Cooking time:
20 minutes

4 **cooking apples**, cored
75 g (2¾ oz) stoned **dates**, chopped
50 g (1¾ oz) **raisins**
50 g (1¾ oz) **pecan nuts**, finely chopped
2 pieces **stem ginger**, finely chopped
4 teaspoons **light muscovado sugar**
25 g (1 oz) **unsalted butter**, softened
1 tablespoon **stem ginger syrup**
1 tablespoon **clear honey**

Preheat the oven to 180ºC/350°F/Gas Mark 4. Line a baking tin with a sheet of non-stick baking parchment. Score the apples lightly around the middle and place in the baking tin.

Mix together the dates, raisins, pecans, stem ginger, sugar and butter. Pack equal amounts into the centre of the apples, pushing down well.

Stir together the stem ginger syrup and honey and spoon it over the dried fruit filling, allowing it to drizzle down inside the apples and slightly over the surface.

Add 3 tablespoons of water to the base of the baking tin and then bake for 20 minutes or until the apples feel soft when the sides are pressed gently. Serve warm.

Tip Do ensure that you have removed all the rough core and that there is sufficient space in the centre of the apples to pack in the stuffing.

Bread & butter pudding

This popular pudding is given a 'makeover' in its contents and preparation. If you prefer, make it in a large dish rather than in individual ones.

Serves 6
Preparation time:
  15 minutes +
  30 minutes soaking
Cooking time:
  30 minutes

50 g (1¾ oz) **unsalted butter**, softened
12 small slices **fruit bread**
lime marmalade
grated zest of a **lime**
300 ml (10 fl oz) **single cream**, plus extra to serve
300 ml (10 fl oz) **semi-skimmed milk**
2 large **eggs**
2 large **egg yolks**
25 g (1 oz) **granulated sugar**

Butter the fruit bread slices and then spread with lime marmalade. Cut the slices into about three pieces each. Grease and base line six ramekin dishes. Layer the bread in the dishes.

Whisk together the lime zest, cream, milk, eggs, egg yolks and sugar and strain through a sieve into a jug. Pour the custard over the bread and leave to soak for 30 minutes. Preheat the oven to 180°C/350°F/Gas Mark 4.

Bake for about 30 minutes, until the custard has set. Allow to cool a little.

Meanwhile, heat 1–2 tablespoons of the marmalade and sieve to remove any peel.

Run a knife around the edges of the puddings to loosen and invert into the centre of serving plates. Remove any lining paper and brush the tops with the marmalade glaze. Serve with single cream.

Strawberry cheesecake

This would make a stunning dessert for a summer dinner party or buffet. The strawberries could be replaced with raspberries.

Serves 10–12
Preparation time:
40 minutes +
3–4 hours chilling

Base
80 g (3 oz) **unsalted butter**, melted
1 tablespoon **golden syrup**
225 g (8 oz) **amaretti biscuits**, crushed

Cheesecake
420 g can **strawberries in light syrup**
11.7 g sachet **gelatine**
500 g (1 lb 2 oz) **ricotta cheese**
250 g (9 oz) **mascarpone cheese**
50 g (1¾ oz) **caster sugar**
2 **eggs**, separated

Topping
3 tablespoons **strawberry conserve**
2 tablespoons **amaretti liqueur**
175 g (6 oz) fresh **strawberries**

Lightly grease a 20 cm (8 inch) springform tin and make the base by combining all the base ingredients. Press them into the tin with a potato masher and chill while you make the cheesecake.

Drain the strawberries, reserving 150 ml (5 fl oz) of the syrup. Place the syrup in a bowl, sprinkle over the gelatine and leave to soak for a minute. Stand the bowl over a pan of hot water and stir until the gelatine has dissolved, or microwave on high for 1 minute and then set to one side to cool.

Liquidise the canned strawberries. In a large bowl, beat the strawberry purée with the cheeses, sugar and egg yolks. Add the cooled gelatine.

In a separate large clean bowl, whisk the egg whites until stiff and then fold them into the strawberry mixture – it is best to fold in 1 tablespoon of the whites to loosen the mixture before adding the remainder. Spoon over the biscuit base and chill for 3–4 hours, until set.

Remove from the tin to a pretty serving plate. Warm the conserve and liqueur together over a gentle heat and then sieve to make a clear glaze. Cut or slice the fresh strawberries and arrange on top of the cheesecake in an attractive pattern. Brush the glaze over the strawberries.

Summer fruit roulade

Roulades are well worth the effort because they look so impressive. A fruit coulis, such as raspberry, would make a perfect accompaniment.

Serves 6–8
Preparation time:
  25 minutes +
  10 minutes cooling
Cooking time:
  15 minutes

Roulade
4 large **eggs**
115 g (4¼ oz) **caster sugar**, plus extra for sprinkling
115 g (4¼ oz) **plain flour**
½ teaspoon **baking powder**
25 g (1 oz) **unsalted butter**, melted and cooled
grated zest of an **orange**

Filling
300 ml (10 fl oz) **double cream**, whipped
175 g (6 oz) **summer fruit**, such as **raspberries**, **strawberries** and **redcurrants**, prepared as necessary

Preheat the oven to 190°C/375°F/Gas Mark 5. Line a 30 × 23 cm (12 × 9 inch) Swiss roll tin with non-stick baking parchment or greased greaseproof paper.

Place the eggs and sugar in a large bowl and whisk until the mixture becomes thick and creamy and the whisk leaves a heavy trail when lifted. Sift the flour and baking powder together and then sift over the egg mixture. Fold in the flour quickly with a metal spoon, followed by the butter and the orange zest. Pour into the prepared tin and gently spread into the corners until the surface is even.

Bake in the oven for about 15 minutes until the surface is golden brown and springs back when gently pressed and the sides have begun to shrink back from the tin.

While the cake is cooking, cut a piece of greaseproof paper slightly larger than the tin and sprinkle generously with caster sugar.

When cooked, invert the cake immediately on to the sugared paper, trim the edges and fold over one of the short edges by 2.5 cm (1 inch). Roll up the roulade, with the paper inside, and fold back the top of the paper so that it doesn't stick to the cake as it cools. Leave to cool for about 10 minutes. Unroll carefully and remove the paper.

Spread most of the cream over the roulade, but not right to the edges, and scatter over the fruit, reserving a few perfect berries to decorate. Roll up the filled roulade and transfer to a serving platter, preferably an oval one.

Spoon the remaining cream into a piping bag and pipe rosettes on top of the roulade. Decorate with some more fruit and serve straight away.

Blackcurrant almond torte

This torte is a cross between a crumble and a shortcake. You can vary the fruit according to taste and availability.

Serves 6–8
Preparation time:
  25 minutes
Cooking time:
  30–40 minutes

150 g (5½ oz) **plain flour**
1 teaspoon **ground cinnamon**
150 g (5½ oz) **caster sugar**
100 g (3½ oz) **ground almonds**
50 g (1¾ oz) **ground rice**
175 g (6 oz) **unsalted butter,** cubed
3 **eggs**, lightly beaten
300 g (10½ oz) **blackcurrants**, fresh or frozen

To serve
icing sugar, sifted
clotted cream

Preheat the oven to 180°C/350°F/Gas Mark 4. Butter the base and sides of a 23 cm (9 inch) springform or loose-bottomed tin and line the sides with non-stick baking parchment or greased greaseproof paper.

Sift the flour and cinnamon together into a large bowl and then stir in the caster sugar, ground almonds and ground rice. Add the butter and rub into the flour mixture until it resembles breadcrumbs. Pour in the eggs and mix together until there are no dry ingredients, being careful not to overmix.

Spread just over half the mixture over the base of the prepared tin. Sprinkle on the blackcurrants and then dot with tablespoons of the remaining mixture. Use a palette knife to spread the mixture to cover the blackcurrants (don't worry if some are still visible though).

Bake for 30–40 minutes, or until it is golden brown and firm to the touch. Leave to cool for 10 minutes before removig from the tin. Dust with icing sugar and serve with a dollop of clotted cream.

Tip If you are using frozen fruit, there is no need to thaw it beforehand.

Pink rhubarb fool

Forced or champagne rhubarb, the beautiful pink spears that are in the shops in early spring, is best for this recipe.

Serves 4
**Preparation and
  cooking time:
  30 minutes +
  20 minutes cooling**

450 g (1 lb) **forced rhubarb**,
  cut into chunks
1–3 tablespoons **clear
  honey**, to taste
juice of an **orange**
250 g tub **Quark**
stem ginger, sliced,
  to decorate
oat biscuits, to serve

Preheat the oven to 190°C/375°F/Gas Mark 5.

Put the rhubarb in an ovenproof dish with the honey and orange juice.

Cook in the oven for 15–20 minutes until the rhubarb is soft. It will make its own juice. Leave to cool.

Put the cooled rhubarb and all the juices in a food processor or blender. Add the Quark and pulse gently to mix. Pile into serving glasses, decorate with slices of stem ginger and serve with oat biscuits.

Lemon meringue tarts

This version of lemon meringue pie takes advantage of convenience foods but tastes totally homemade. Serve with fresh raspberries.

Serves 6
Preparation time:
  15 minutes
Cooking time:
  35–40 minutes

6 **ready-made sweet pastry cases**
6 tablespoons good-quality **lemon curd**
grated zest of 2 **lemons**
juice of a **lemon**
2 large **egg yolks**
3 large **egg whites**
125 g (4½ oz) **caster sugar**

Preheat the oven to 150°C/300°F/Gas Mark 2. Place the pastry cases on a baking tray.

Put the lemon curd, lemon zest, lemon juice and egg yolks in a bowl and mix until all the ingredients are combined. Divide the mixture between the pastry cases.

In a separate large clean bowl, whisk the egg whites until they are stiff and then add the sugar, a teaspoon at a time, while continuing to whisk. Spoon the mixture into a large piping bag fitted with a large star nozzle.

Pipe the meringue on to the lemon filling, starting with the edges and finishing with a peak in the centre (you could simply spoon the meringue on top and 'fluff' into a peak with a palette knife).

Bake in the oven for 35–40 minutes, until the meringue is crisp and golden brown. Serve warm or cold.

Mango & lime syllabub

Mangoes have a natural affinity with limes. However, vary the fruit to suit your tastes. Serve with crisp dessert biscuits.

Serves 4–6
Preparation time:
   20 minutes + at least
   30 minutes chilling

grated zest and juice of
   2 **limes**
2 tablespoons **sherry**
2 tablespoons **brandy**
2 tablespoons **icing sugar**
2 large ripe **mangoes**,
   peeled and stoned, or
   2 × 425 g cans **mango
   slices**, drained
230 ml (8 fl oz) **double cream**

Mix the lime zest and juice into the sherry, brandy and sugar and set aside.

Put the mango flesh into a food processor and blend to make a purée. Divide the purée between tall serving glasses and place in the fridge to chill.

Place the cream in a bowl and strain the brandy mixture over it, discarding the zest.

Whisk it until soft peaks form (be careful not to over whisk as the mixture will continue to thicken in the fridge). Spoon or pipe over the mango purée. Cover with cling film and return to the fridge for at least 30 minutes or until ready to serve.

Tip You could create a mango and lime ice cream by folding the mango purée into the syllabub mixture and freezing – there is no need to beat the mixture while it is freezing.

Apricot & brandy trifle

Thankfully, trifles have regained their popularity. You can cheat a little in this recipe by using ready-made custard.

Serves 6–8
Preparation time:
  40 minutes + 2 hours chilling

24 ready-to-eat **dried apricots**
150 ml (5 fl oz) fresh **orange juice**
5 tablespoons **brandy**
1 packet **trifle sponges**
apricot conserve
500 g carton **ready-made custard**
300 ml (10 fl oz) **whipping cream**, whipped

To decorate
toasted flaked almonds
ready-to-eat **dried apricots**, chopped

Place the apricots and orange juice in a small lidded saucepan, bring to the boil and simmer very gently, covered, for 15–20 minutes, until very tender. Add the brandy and allow to cool.

Split the sponges in half horizontally and spread generously with the apricot conserve. Sandwich together again and cut into cubes. Put in the base of a glass trifle bowl and spoon the apricots and all the orange and brandy juices on top. Pour the custard on top and level the surface.

Spread two-thirds of the cream over the custard and spoon the remainder into a piping bag fitted with a star nozzle. Sprinkle the surface with the flaked almonds. Pipe cream rosettes around the edges and decorate them with dried apricot pieces. Chill for a couple of hours.

Eton mess

This is quite delicious and incredibly easy to make. The raspberry coulis gives it an interesting dimension.

Serves 4
Preparation time:
  10 minutes

250 g (9 oz) **ricotta cheese**
150 g (5½ oz) **Greek yogurt**
4 **meringue nests**, roughly
  crushed
225 g (8 oz) **strawberries**,
  hulled and quartered,
  plus extra to decorate
  (optional)
190 g jar **raspberry coulis**

Place the ricotta cheese and yogurt in a large bowl and mix well.

Layer the ricotta mixture with the crushed meringues and quartered strawberries in four glass dessert dishes, drizzling the raspberry coulis in between the layers.

Decorate with extra strawberries, if using, and serve straight away.

Raspberry crème brulée

This tastes as if it has been made the traditional way but takes just a few minutes. You could substitute any other soft fruit for the raspberries.

Serves 4
Preparation time:
  **15 minutes + at least
  2 hours chilling**

250 g (9 oz) fresh
  raspberries
250 g (9 oz) **ready-made
  vanilla custard**
250 g (9 oz) **crème fraîche**
2–3 tablespoons **caster
  sugar**

Divide the raspberries between four 200 ml (7 fl oz) flameproof dishes.

Mix together the custard and crème fraîche and then carefully spoon the mixture on to the raspberries and flatten the surface. Chill for at least 2 hours.

Sprinkle the surfaces generously with the caster sugar and caramelise using a cook's blowtorch, or put under a hot grill to caramelise. Serve straight away.

White chocolate soufflés

Most people shy away from making a hot soufflé as they think it's far too difficult. This recipe cheats a little by using ready-made custard.

Serves 6
Preparation time:
 25 minutes
Cooking time:
 15–20 minutes

25 g (1 oz) **unsalted butter,**
 melted
1 tablespoon **caster sugar**
500 g (1 lb 2 oz) **ready-made
 custard**
1 **vanilla pod**
100 g (3½ oz) **white
 chocolate,** melted
4 large **eggs,** separated
150 ml (5 fl oz) **double
 cream,** whipped
cocoa powder,
 sifted, to decorate

Preheat the oven to 200°C/400°F/Gas Mark 6. Place a baking tray in the oven. Brush the melted butter generously on the inside of six individual 175 ml (6 fl oz) soufflé dishes. Dust the buttered surfaces with the caster sugar.

Spoon the custard into a large bowl, split the vanilla pod lengthways and scrape the seeds into the custard. Pour in the melted white chocolate and stir to combine. Add the egg yolks, one at a time, stirring after each addition. Fold in the cream.

Whisk the egg whites in a large clean bowl until they are stiff. Fold a spoonful of the whites into the chocolate mixture using a large metal spoon to loosen it, and then fold in the remainder using a figure-of-eight action. Quickly spoon the soufflé mixture into the prepared dishes and run your little finger around the edge of the soufflés to help them rise well as they cook.

Place the dishes on the preheated tray and bake for 15–20 minutes until well risen, golden and still very slightly soft in the centre. Sprinkle with cocoa and serve immediately.

Tip You can make most of the recipe (up to the egg whites) up to about an hour in advance. The recipe can be completed just before you sit down to your main course.

Sticky mocha puddings

This version of sticky toffee pudding is very chocolatey and the butterscotch sauce complements it well. Serve with crème fraîche or vanilla ice cream.

Serves 6
Preparation time:
  40 minutes
Cooking time:
  35–40 minutes

115 g (4¼ oz) stoned **dates**, chopped
½ teaspoon **bicarbonate of soda**
1 heaped teaspoon **instant coffee granules**
50 g (1¾ oz) **unsalted butter**, softened
115 g (4¼ oz) **caster sugar**
2 **eggs**, beaten
150 g (5½ oz) **self-raising flour**
1 tablespoon **cocoa powder**
80 g (3 oz) **plain chocolate**, broken into small pieces
80 g (3 oz) **walnut pieces**

Butterscotch sauce
80 g (3 oz) **dark muscovado sugar**
80 g (3 oz) **unsalted butter**, cubed
150 ml (5 fl oz) **double cream**

Put the dates in a saucepan with 150 ml (5 fl oz) of water, the bicarbonate of soda and coffee, bring to the boil and then leave to stand for 10 minutes.

Preheat the oven to 180°C/350°F/Gas Mark 4. Place a roasting tin half filled with water in the oven. Grease and base line six 250 ml (8 fl oz) pudding moulds with discs of non-stick baking parchment or greased greaseproof paper.

Cream the butter with the sugar until light and fluffy, and then gradually beat in the eggs. Sift the flour and cocoa together and fold into the mixture. Fold in the remaining ingredients, including the dates and their soaking liquid, mix well and divide between the moulds. (It will look very wet at this stage.)

Bake for 35–40 minutes until risen and firm to the touch – you may need to cover the tops with a sheet of foil towards the end of the cooking to prevent the tops from burning.

While they are cooking, make the butterscotch sauce. Place all the ingredients in a saucepan and stir until the sugar dissolves. Bring to the boil and boil for 2–3 minutes, stirring from time to time.

To serve, run a knife around the edges of the puddings and turn out on to serving plates. Remove the paper discs. Pour the sauce over the tops and serve straight away.

Chocolate mocha mousse

A delicious and not too rich mousse, serve in pretty coffee cups and decorate with chocolate coated coffee beans for an impressive dessert.

Serves 4–6
Preparation and cooking time:
20 minutes +
1½–2 hours setting

100 g (3½ oz) **plain chocolate** (at least 70% cocoa solids), broken into pieces
2 tablespoons **strong coffee**
3 **eggs**, separated
250 g (9 oz) **Quark**, at room temperature
25 g (1 oz) **caster sugar**
chocolate curls, to decorate

Melt the chocolate in a small bowl over a pan of hot water. Stir in the coffee and the egg yolks and mix well. Set aside to cool slightly. In a large clean bowl, whisk the egg whites until they are stiff but not dry.

Place the Quark in a bowl and stir until smooth, adding the caster sugar. Carefully stir in the chocolate mixture until well combined. It's important that the Quark is almost at room temperature because if it is used straight from the fridge its coldness will cause the chocolate to 'set' and they will not combine smoothly.

Stir one spoonful of the egg whites into the mixture to loosen it up, and then gently fold in the rest taking care not to knock out any of the volume.

Divide the mousse between 4–6 ramekin dishes or coffee cups and place in the fridge for 1½–2 hours to set. Decorate each mousse with a few chocolate curls before serving.

Banana & apricot cake

A moist, loaf-type cake that is good in lunchboxes or for picnics. Make sure the bananas are really ripe to allow their flavour to come through.

Makes 12 slices
Preparation time:
  20 minutes + cooling
Baking time:
  45–50 minutes

100 g (3½ oz) **margarine**
100 g (3½ oz) **soft light
  brown sugar**
2 **eggs**, lightly beaten
75 g (2¾ oz) **walnuts**,
  roughly chopped
50 g (1¾ oz) ready-to-eat
  dried apricots, roughly
  chopped
2 **bananas**, mashed
½ teaspoon **mixed spice**
225 g (8 oz) **self-raising flour**

Preheat the oven to 180°C/350°F/Gas Mark 4. Grease a 900 g (2 lb) loaf tin and base line with non-stick baking parchment or greased greaseproof paper.

Cream the margarine and sugar together until light and fluffy, and then gradually beat in the eggs.

Reserve a quarter of the chopped walnuts and fold the rest into the creamed mixture along with the apricots and mashed bananas. Fold in the mixed spice and flour.

Transfer the mixture to the prepared tin, level the surface and sprinkle over the reserved chopped walnuts.

Bake in the oven for 45–50 minutes until risen, golden and firm to the touch. A skewer inserted into the middle of the cake should come out clean.

Allow to cool in the tin for 5 minutes and then turn out on to a wire rack to cool completely. Cut into slices for serving.

Spiced orange teabread

This is a lovely moist teabread, full of flavour. The flavour actually improves on keeping, but wrap it in foil to keep it from drying out.

Makes 12–14 slices
Preparation time:
10 minutes +
overnight soaking
+ cooling
Baking time:
1–1¼ hours

150 g (5½ oz) **sultanas**
150 g (5½ oz) **raisins**
50 g (1¾ oz) **mixed chopped**
peel
grated zest and juice of an
orange
175 g (6 oz) **soft light brown**
sugar
about 200 ml (7 fl oz) hot
strong **tea**
300 g (10½ oz) **self-raising**
wholemeal flour
1 teaspoon **mixed spice**
1 **egg**, lightly beaten
demerara sugar, for
sprinkling

Place the dried fruit, mixed peel, orange zest and sugar into a medium-sized bowl. Pour the orange juice into a measuring jug and add sufficient tea to make 300 ml (10 fl oz) of liquid. Pour this over the fruit and stir well to dissolve the sugar. Cover the bowl and leave overnight to allow the fruit to swell.

Preheat the oven to 150°C/300°F/Gas Mark 2. Grease a 900 g (2 lb) loaf tin and base line with non-stick baking parchment or greased greaseproof paper.

Stir the flour, mixed spice and beaten egg into the fruit mixture. Mix thoroughly, and then transfer into the loaf tin and level the surface. Sprinkle the top with a little demerara sugar.

Bake in the oven for 1–1¼ hours until risen and firm to the touch. A skewer inserted into the middle of the loaf should come out clean. Leave to cool in the tin for 10 minutes, and then turn out on to a wire rack to cool completely. Cut into slices for serving.

Carrot cake

This is popular at many sandwich and coffee bars and is always a welcome ingredient in lunchboxes – for big and little people.

Makes 12 squares
Preparation and baking time: 60–65 minutes + cooling

225 g (8 oz) **self-raising flour**
1½ teaspoons **baking powder**
1 tablespoon **mixed spice**
1 teaspoon **ground ginger**
175 g (6 oz) **golden caster sugar**
3 large **eggs**, beaten
200 ml (7 fl oz) **sunflower oil**
½ teaspoon **vanilla extract**
50 g (1¾ oz) **walnut halves**, roughly chopped
225 g (8 oz) grated **carrot**
12 **walnut halves**, to decorate

Icing
175 g (6 oz) **low fat cream cheese**
25 g (1 oz) **unsalted butter**, softened
80 g (3 oz) **icing sugar**, sifted
lemon juice
vanilla extract

Preheat the oven to 180°C/350°F/Gas Mark 4. Grease a shallow 17 × 26 cm (6½ × 10½ inch) tin and line with non-stick baking parchment or greased greaseproof paper.

In a large bowl, sift together the flour, baking powder and spices. Stir in the sugar.

Make a well in the centre and add the eggs, oil and vanilla extract. Stir until smooth. Mix in the walnuts and carrot and spoon into the prepared tin. Level the surface.

Bake the cake in the centre of the oven for 40–45 minutes until a metal skewer inserted in the middle comes out clean. Allow to cool in tin for 10 minutes before turning out on to a wire rack to cool completely.

To make the icing, beat together the cream cheese and butter until smooth. Gradually add the sifted icing sugar, followed by a squeeze of lemon juice and a few drops of vanilla extract to taste.

Spread the icing evenly over the cake's surface. Mark into 12 squares and decorate each with a walnut half. Store in the fridge, covered, to prevent it from drying out.

Boston brownies

This is scrumptious example of American influence. These moist squares are packed with nuts, though you could substitute chocolate drops instead.

Makes 15
Preparation time:
  20 minutes + cooling
Baking time:
  25–30 minutes

115 g (4¼ oz) **plain chocolate** (at least 70% cocoa solids), broken into pieces

115 g (4¼ oz) **unsalted butter** or **margarine**, cubed

2 large **eggs**, beaten

1 teaspoon **vanilla extract**

100 g (3½ oz) **macadamia nuts**, chopped

50 g (1¼ oz) **plain flour**

½ teaspoon **baking powder**

Preheat the oven to 180°C/350°F/Gas Mark 4. Grease and line a shallow 28 × 18 cm (11 × 7 inch) baking tin.

Melt the chocolate and butter or margarine in a bowl set over a pan of hot water. Remove from the heat, stir until smooth and then leave to cool slightly.

Whisk in the beaten eggs and vanilla extract and stir in three-quarters of the nuts. Sift together the flour and baking powder and fold in.

Pour into the prepared tin and shake to level the surface. Sprinkle the reserved nuts evenly over the top and place on the middle shelf of the oven. Bake for 25–30 minutes, until the middle is just firm (it does continue to cook slightly when taken out of the oven) and the mixture has started to come away from the edges of the tin.

Cool in tin for 10 minutes before cutting into 15 squares and transferring to a wire rack to cool completely.

Fruit loaf

A traditional fruit bread made with mixed dried fruit that tastes equally good toasted, with lots of butter.

Makes 1 × 900 g (2 lb) loaf
Preparation time: 25–30 minutes + rising + cooling
Baking time: 25–35 minutes

150 ml (5 fl oz) hand-hot **semi-skimmed milk**
25 g (1 oz) **caster sugar**, plus 1 teaspoon
15 g (½ oz) **dried yeast**
450 g (1 lb) **strong white flour**
1 teaspoon **salt**
25 g (1 oz) **margarine**
175 g (6 oz) **mixed dried fruit**

Mix together 150 ml (5 fl oz) of hand-hot water with the milk and dissolve the teaspoon of sugar in the liquid. Sprinkle in the yeast and stir to mix. Leave in a warm place for 10–15 minutes, until frothy.

Sift the flour and salt into a bowl, rub in the margarine and add the remaining sugar. Stir in the dried fruit. Add the yeast mixture and mix to form a soft dough.

Knead the dough on a lightly floured surface until smooth and elastic. Place in a clean, greased bowl, cover and leave to rise until doubled in size (the time will depend on the warmth of your room).

Turn out the dough on to a lightly floured surface, knock back and knead again. Shape and place in a 900 g (2 lb) greased loaf tin. Cover and leave to prove for 30 minutes. Preheat the oven to 200°C/400°F/Gas Mark 6.

Bake the loaf for 25–35 minutes, until golden and hollow-sounding when tapped on the base. Transfer to a wire rack to cool.

Blueberry friands

These are very easy to make as they only require mixing, so why not let the children have a go – they are the next generation of cooks after all.

Makes 12
Preparation time:
 20 minutes + cooling
Baking time:
 25–30 minutes

80 g (3 oz) **unsalted butter** or
 margarine
225 g (8 oz) **plain flour**
2 teaspoons **baking powder**
½ teaspoon **bicarbonate of
 soda**
115 g (4¼ oz) **golden
 granulated sugar**, plus 2
 teaspoons for sprinkling
225 ml (8 fl oz) **natural bio
 yogurt**
1 large **egg**, beaten
½ teaspoon **vanilla extract**
175 g (6 oz) **blueberries**,
 washed and dried

Preheat the oven to 180°C/350°F/Gas Mark 4. Set out 12 paper muffin cases in a muffin tin or grease the holes and base line with non-stick baking parchment or greased greaseproof paper.

Melt the butter or margarine and allow to cool slightly. Sift the flour, baking powder and bicarbonate of soda into a large bowl. Stir in the sugar.

Make a well in the centre of the dry ingredients and add the melted butter, yogurt, beaten egg and vanilla extract. Stir to just combine. The mixture will look lumpy – this is fine – over mixing will make the friands heavy and tough.

Carefully fold in the blueberries, taking care not to break them up. Divide between the muffin cases or holes and sprinkle a little sugar over the top of each.

Bake in the centre of the oven for 25–30 minutes, until the friands are risen and crisp on the top. Cover with foil towards the end if they are browning too much. Turn out on a wire rack to cool or eat warm.

Chelsea buns

A traditional recipe for this sweet bun. A real old English favourite filled with jewel-like mixed fruit.

Makes 12
Preparation and baking time:
50–60 minutes + rising + cooling

2 teaspoons **dried yeast**
½ teaspoon **caster sugar**
5 tablespoons hand-hot **semi-skimmed milk**
50 g (1¾ oz) **strong white flour**

Dough
175 g (6 oz) **strong white flour**
½ teaspoon **salt**
25 g (1 oz) **caster sugar**
25 g (1 oz) **margarine**
1 **egg**, beaten

Filling
25 g (1 oz) **unsalted butter**, melted
115 g (4¼ oz) **mixed dried fruit**
50 g (1¾ oz) **light muscovado sugar**
½ teaspoon **ground cinnamon**

To make the yeast batter, place the yeast and sugar in a small jug. Stir in the milk and leave for 5 minutes. Stir in the flour and leave in a warm place until frothy (about 15–20 minutes).

To make the dough, sift together the flour and salt and mix in the sugar. Rub in the margarine. Stir in the egg and the yeast batter and mix to give a soft dough.

Turn out on to a lightly floured surface and knead for 8–10 minutes, until the dough is smooth, elastic and no longer sticky. Place the dough in a clean, greased bowl, cover and leave to rise until doubled in size (the time will depend on the warmth of your room).

Transfer the risen dough to a lightly floured surface and knock back and knead. Roll the dough into a rectangle 30 × 23 cm (12 × 9 inches). Brush the surface with the melted butter and sprinkle with the fruit, sugar and cinnamon.

Roll up the dough like a Swiss roll, starting at the longest side. Cut into 12 equal pieces and place in a 17 × 26 cm (6½ × 10½ inch) greased tin, cut-side down. Cover with greased cling film and leave to prove for about 30 minutes until well risen. Preheat the oven to 220°C/ 425°F/Gas Mark 7.

Bake for 20–25 minutes, until golden brown. Turn out on to a wire rack to cool.

Plain scones

This recipe can be used as a base for either sweet or savoury scones.
Don't over handle the dough as this will cause it to be tough and solid.

Makes about 15 scones
Preparation time:
  10–15 minutes +
  cooling
Baking time:
  10–15 minutes

450 g (1 lb) **self-raising flour,**
  plus extra for dusting
115 g (4¼ oz) **margarine**
50 g (1¾ oz) **caster sugar**
  (for a sweet scone dough)
175–225 ml (6–8 fl oz) **milk,**
  plus extra for brushing

Preheat the oven to 220°C/425°F/Gas Mark 7.

Sift the flour into a mixing bowl and rub in the margarine until the mixture resembles fine breadcrumbs. Stir in the sugar if making a sweet dough.

Make a well in the centre and stir in enough milk to give a fairly soft dough.

Turn on to a floured surface and knead lightly to remove any cracks. Roll out to about 2 cm (¾ inch) thick and use a cutter to cut out 5 cm (2 inch) rounds. Knead the remaining dough and re-roll and cut. Place the scones on a greased baking tray and glaze with a little milk.

Bake until well risen and golden brown, about 10–15 minutes. Transfer to a wire rack to cool and sprinkle with a little flour if liked.

Traditional flapjacks

A favourite biscuit that is easy to make. A great store-cupboard standby and a delicious teatime treat for children.

Makes 16
Preparation time:
   10–15 minutes +
   cooling
Baking time:
   20–25 minutes

200 g (7 oz) **unsalted butter**
6 tablespoons **golden syrup**
80 g (3 oz) **light muscovado**
   sugar
350 g (12 oz) **rolled oats**

Preheat the oven to 190°C/375°F/Gas Mark 5.

Heat the butter, syrup and sugar in a saucepan until the butter has melted. Add the rolled oats and mix well. Press into a greased 18 × 30 cm (7 × 12 inch) tin.

Bake for 20–25 minutes, until golden.

Mark into bars and leave to cool before removing from the tin. Store in an airtight container for up to a week.

Tip Keep an eye on these at the end of their cooking time, as if the flapjacks are overcooked, they won't have that delicious soft texture.

Index